Wilderness Above the Sound

Wilderness Above the Sound

The Story of Mount Rainier National Park

by Arthur D. Martinson
Foreword by Alfred Runte

NORTHLAND PRESS ❧ FLAGSTAFF, ARIZONA

TABLE OF CONTENTS

Summit guides, Rainier National Park Company, n.d.
Photo by Asahel Curtis. Courtesy University of Washington.

To my parents, Al and Mabel Martinson, who first took me and my brothers and sisters to Mount Rainier for picknicking and camping; and to my wife, Marilyn, and our children, Chad and Stacey, with whom I have spent many memorable times hiking the park's trails.

Visitors enjoying the scenery from Paradise Valley.
Rotary Club "Mt. Tacoma Trip," August 25-26, 1911.
Photo by R. R. Raymoth. Courtesy Washington State Historical Society.

"The mountain stands alone,
and in the distance it declares
it's awesome solitary existence.
It's spirit is the very soul
of the Northwest."

SUE KOETEEUW
from *Moods of the Mountain*
by Josef Scaylea
Superior Publishing, 1981

Mount Rainier from
Edith Creek in Paradise Valley.
Photo by Kirkendall/Spring, 1973.

Mt. Rainier from Puget Sound. *Photo by Josef Scaylea.*

FOREWORD

If asked to list the distinctive contributions of their country to world civilization, most Americans undoubtedly would miss one of the most significant: the national park idea. Mount Rainier, the nation's fifth national park, is the subject of this lively, provocative book by Arthur D. Martinson. The establishment of Mount Rainier National Park in 1899 came at the close of a century of growing public awareness about threats to the nation's forests, wildlife, and natural landmarks. As early as 1864, Congress set aside California's fabled Yosemite Valley and a nearby grove of giant sequoias for "public use, resort, and recreation," each to be held "inalienable for all time." Donation of the two tracts to California for management cost Yosemite

Valley the honor of being called the first *national* park, but the protection of both wonders by an act of Congress was clearly undertaken in the interest of the American people as a whole. The national park idea—in fact if not in name—had been born.

As the author notes, the development of national parks in the nineteenth century cannot be ascribed to ecological concerns. As a science, the practice of ecology is a twentieth-century phenomenon. More to the point, Americans of the nineteenth century—Mount Rainier's defenders among them—were alarmed by the prospect of losing the great natural wonders of the American West to private exploitation. In private control, Yosemite Valley and the giant sequoias, for example, would be robbed of their credibility as symbols of national pride and achievement. For decades American artists, writers, and other intellectuals had suffered the embarrassment of representing a society that lacked world-renowned cultural attainments. In contrast to the storied cultures and landmarks of Europe, the United States, especially in its infancy, had no great "monuments" of literary or artistic fame. As the noted British critic Sydney Smith asked derisively in 1820, "In the four quarters of the globe, who reads an American book? or goes to an American play? or looks at an American picture or statue?" Smith's insulting tone aside, his point was still well taken: in terms of cultural heritage, at least, the United States of the early nineteenth century indeed had yet to prove itself.

World class American literature, art, and architecture, of course, would be decades, even centuries, in the making. In the meantime, although America lacked great artistic achievements, the country by no means lacked scenic beauty. Thanks to a combination of diplomacy and conquest, the young nation stretched from sea to sea by 1848. While it could be argued that the far West was still culturally barren, unlike the East, its natural features were truly unparalleled. Yosemite, the giant sequoias, Yellowstone, and the Grand Canyon—among other "wonderlands" of the American West—reassured the young nation of its own claims to a long and romantic antiquity. That antiquity simply had to be measured in natural rather than human time. America had ancient monuments and linkages to the past, it was just that Americans found them in the monuments of nature rather than in the monuments of human endeavor.

The establishment of Yellowstone National Park, Wyoming, approved March 1, 1872, conclusively demonstrated to the United States the potential cultural significance of scenic preservation. Congressional action again followed the realization that Yellowstone's geysers, canyons, and waterfalls otherwise would fall victim to private claimants, exploiters whose callous disregard for natural beauty would also jeopardize Yellowstone's reputation as another milepost of cultural identity. Years of congressional indifference followed, but finally, in 1890, the federal government once more responded to appeals to protect representative natural features on the public lands of the West. Congress voted to create Yosemite, Sequoia, and General Grant national parks, all in California's high Sierra. With approximately fifteen hundred square miles, Yosemite Valley was by far the largest of the three, although it and Mariposa Redwood Grove remained in state ownership until 1906.

Precedent was now firmly established for the protection of Mount Rainier in Washington State. Rising majestically above the forests, lakes, and farmlands of the Puget Sound country, the mountain appealed to every fantasy of the American imagination. "I remember as I first watched it grow," wrote Carl Synder, an early park advocate, "luminous, opalescent, and regal from out the mantle of mist which held it as a shroud. I could have summoned back the whole antique world of mythology and domiciled it upon this greater and grander Olympus,...this St. Peter's of the skies."

The rest is Arthur Martinson's story. Thanks to his dedication and initiative, the essential history of Mount Rainier National Park has finally been brought to life. I applaud his effort, which includes one of the most graphic selections of historical photographs ever brought together in a single park history. Regrettably, the future of Mount Rainier National Park—not to mention the parks nationwide—cannot be taken for granted. I therefore hope this book will do more than introduce the history of this fascinating landmark. Perhaps it will inspire readers to help preserve all of America's national parks in the spirit of their establishment, "inalienable for all time."

ALFRED RUNTE
University of Washington

ACKNOWLEDGEMENTS

I am indebted to Pacific Lutheran University, particularly President William O. Rieke; Provost Richard Jungkuntz; and Dean David A. Atkinson, Social Sciences, for their support in granting a Regency Advancement Award to be used in the preparation of this book. To my colleagues in the history department, the cooperative education office, and at East Campus, I extend my thanks for their enthusiasm and vocal support. A special thanks to Linda Rhoades-Kendrick for typing the manuscript.

Tony King, director of the Washington State Historical Society, staff members Frank Green, Elaine Webster, and photographer Richard Frederick provided timely assistance in securing photographic reproductions. Likewise, Gary Reese, director of the Northwest Room, Tacoma Public Library, tracked regional historical facts, and Ronald Fields, director of the Permanent Collection at the University of Puget Sound, gave generously of his time and expertise in providing access to historical paintings of the mountain.

National park personnel, including the late Daniel J. Tobin, Pacific Northwest regional director; Bob Dunnagan, assistant superintendent for natural resource planning at Mount Rainier National Park; and Bill Dengler, chief park naturalist, also at

Mountain climbers approaching Columbia Crest crater (14,410 ft.), the highest point on the summit of Mount Rainier. *Photo by Bob and Ira Spring, 1972.*

Mount Rainier, were most helpful in offering information and viewpoints on the status of current management issues and concerns.

I owe much to Alfred Runte, who not only lent his editing expertise to the manuscript, but also helped locate research material through the generous assistance of personnel associated with the Pacific Northwest Collection, University of Washington. In addition, Al was instrumental in securing photographic reproductions from Burlington Northern, Inc., headquarters, Seattle, Washington. Burlington Northern administrative personnel, particularly Ernie Bisset and Allan Boyce, were especially helpful.

Finally, to the many friends who worked at Mount Rainier as trailmen, rangers, guides, or concessionaire employees, I thank you for some of the fondest memories of my life. Together, we shared an exhilarating experience.

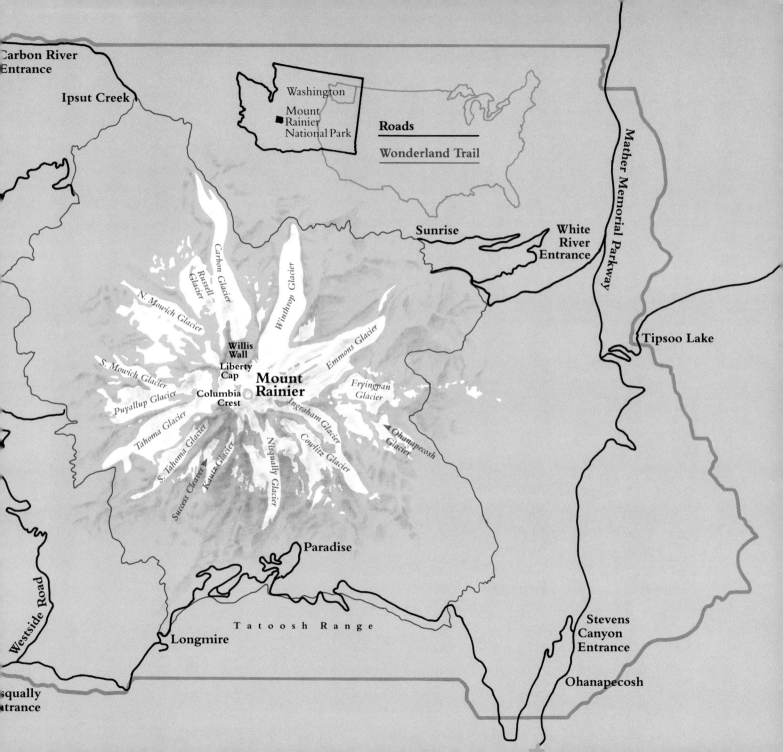

Carbon River
Entrance

Ipsut Creek

Washington

Mount
Rainier
National Park

Roads

Wonderland Trail

Sunrise

White
River
Entrance

Mather Memorial Parkway

Tipsoo Lake

Carbon Glacier

Russell Glacier

Winthrop Glacier

N. Mowich Glacier

Emmons Glacier

**Willis
Wall**

**Liberty
Cap**

S. Mowich Glacier

Fryingpan Glacier

**Columbia
Crest**

**Mount
Rainier**

Puyallup Glacier

Ingraham Glacier

Tahoma Glacier

Ohanapecosh Glacier

S. Tahoma Glacier

Cowlitz Glacier

Success Cleaver

Kautz Glacier

Nisqually Glacier

Paradise

Westside Road

T a t o o s h   R a n g e

Longmire

Stevens
Canyon
Entrance

squally
trance

Ohanapecosh

Mount Rainier from upper Paradise Valley. To the right is Nisqually Glacier, long a popular tourist attraction.
Photo by Bob and Ira Spring, 1973.

PROLOGUE

A WILDERNESS WORLD

In a region renowned for its breathtaking topography, the dormant volcanic cone of Mount Rainier looms above its surroundings with a singular commanding presence. A full 14,410 feet higher than the nearby tides of Puget Sound, the mountain dwarfs the Cascade Range beneath it, while seemingly standing guard over distant volcanic peaks. For nearly one hundred miles in every direction, Rainier's glacier-capped summit is the most prominent landmark in western Washington State. Seen from these great distances, the mountain creates the illusion, in the words of John Muir, of being "just back of a strip of woods only a mile or two in breadth." Varying light and weather conditions, especially the fiery sunsets of Puget Sound winters, also create different and sometimes awesome summit moods. Occasionally, particularly at dawn or during a bright moonlit evening, the mountain appears as a giant silhouette. Indian folklore referred to such phenomena in godlike terms; the modern observer is likewise captivated by Mount Rainier's ever-changing mystique.

A visit to Mount Rainier National Park invariably reveals more than can be seen from a distance. "So overwhelming is the presence of Mount Rainier," states a park brochure, that "little attention is paid to the park's encircling forest." The contrasts are nonetheless striking as motorists first entering the park pass through towering stands of old growth Douglas fir and other western conifers. Higher up,

1

the changing contrasts in landscape, color, climate, and life zones continue. Above timberline, subalpine meadows and fading patches of plant life abound; higher still there is nothing green, only snow and blue ice, rocks and jagged ridges. Twenty-seven named glaciers, from frozen snowfields to extensive crevasse-laden ice fields up to six miles long, flank the mountain on all sides. The glacier system—largest single peak system in the lower forty-eight states—is the multiple source of rivers that flow through spectacular canyons and valleys before spilling their ice-born waters into Puget Sound and the Columbia River.

Lakes, marshes, forested slopes, and other less dramatic landscapes round out the wilderness world that is Mount Rainier National Park. Within these various environments, wildlife finds refuge from shrinking habitats beyond park borders. Often bear, deer, and elk are sighted along the more than two hundred fifty miles of trails and approximately one hundred fifty miles of paved and gravel roads that provide varying degrees of access to popular viewing points. In late spring and early summer, mountain meadows, at last freed of winter snows, further erupt in a kaleidoscope of color, drawing tens of thousands of wildflower enthusiasts from all across the United States and from many countries of the world.

To be sure, Mount Rainier is predominantly a day-visitor national park. Although many trails lead the wilderness enthusiast to remote corners of the preserve, the panoramic views at the end of mountain roads, most notably at Paradise and Sunrise, draw thousands more visitors who seldom wander beyond sight of their automobiles. Still, whether from campgrounds and parking lots or summit-bound trails, everyone senses the overwhelming presence of the mountain. John Muir himself, following a successful climb to the summit in 1888, conceded that although the view from the top "could hardly be surpassed in sublimity and grandeur," there might be more pleasure in seeing Rainier from its base. Either way, he concluded, fortunate were those "to whom lofty mountain-tops are within reach, for the lights that shine there illumine all that lies below."

In the wake of the violent eruption of Mount St. Helens on May 18, 1980, an even greater sense of Mount Rainier's presence has stirred the public's curiosity. Although Mount Rainier's latest eruptions in the nineteenth century were minor episodes of smoke and ash, the dramatic rebirth of Mount St. Helens proves conclusively that no volcano in the Pacific Northwest should be considered extinct. On Mount Rainier itself, steam vents are constant reminders that thermal processes deep beneath the glaciers are still undoubtedly active. Though even a minor eruption has not occurred in more than a century, the never-ending rumblings and hissings ris-

On the road to Paradise, above Narada Falls. Open auto stages were popular in the 1920s. *Courtesy Special Collections, University of Washington Libraries.*

ing from Rainier's geological depths leave us to ponder when, not if, the next eruption will indeed take place.

Fortunately, America's national parks and wilderness areas are intended as sanctuaries for nature's order, even in its most unstable and violent forms. Meanwhile, the high-country wisdom of John Muir still rings true, just as it did for those first drawn to the grandeur of Mount Rainier and other national parks:

> Climb the mountains and get their good tidings. Nature's peace will flow into you as the sunshine into the trees. The winds will blow their freshness into you, and the storms their energy, while cares will drop off like autumn leaves.

THE
EYES OF
DISCOVERY

Long before the arrival of European and American explorers in the Pacific Northwest, Indians were seasonal inhabitants around the base of Mount Rainier. To them it was Tahoma, or Takhoma, possibly meaning "the great white snowy mountain." In late summer and early fall, bands of natives followed the snowline to subalpine meadows to hunt, pick berries, and conduct ceremonies and games. Chief Owhi of the Yakima Tribe considered Yakima Park—now an auto stop at the end of a scenic road—especially suitable for such purposes. Similar activities, though probably to a lesser degree, were carried on by westside Puyallup and Nisqually Indians at Squaw Lake near Indian Henry's Hunting Ground, and probably in or around Paradise Valley, known to them as *Saghalie Illahe,* the "land of peace."

Presumably, members of at least four tribes frequently made contact with one another on the lower slopes of Mount Rainier. A rock shelter—perhaps 1,000 years old—on Fryingpan Creek, shows evidence of occupation by the Yakimas, even though the shelter's location is well within the traditional area of the Puyallup and Muckleshoot Indians. The discovery of another prehistoric campsite on the south side of the park in upper Stevens Canyon is further evidence of Indian occupation in the areas

Mt. Rainier from Tatoosh Range, 1920. *Photo by Asahel Curtis. Courtesy Washington State Historical Society.*

5

between 2,500 and 6,400 feet.

Among the unanswered questions about Indian discoveries and life in the wilderness surrounding Mount Rainier, the overriding mystery concerns the question of individual or tribal ventures above snowline. Archaeological and historical evidence indicate that such activity rarely occurred, and that the summit itself was never climbed. To the Indian, all great peaks were sacred and not to be violated or desecrated by the defiant footsteps of a climber. "The flames of eruption, the fall of an avalanche, told the wrath of the mountain god," wrote John H. Williams in his book *The Mountain That Was "God."* The only exceptions to this belief are found in native folklore. Several legends refer to conquests of the summit by medicine men and other individuals. One of these legends describes how a Yakima Indian discovered a "summit lake," which then spilled over and rushed down the mountainside into the area where the small town of Orting now stands. Another legend describes the Indians' version of the Great Flood, similar to the biblical account. The Great Spirit lived on the summit of Takhoma, where he instructed a good and wise man to make a long "rope of arrows" extending far below to the foothills. All the good people and good animals climbed up that rope, while all of the evil people and animals were left behind to drown as the earth became inundated with water. Some time later the waters receded, and so the good people descended the mountain with their animals to resume life on earth once again.

Still another legend identifies an Indian named Jamaiakan who claimed to a fur trader that he had conquered Mount Rainier. This tale is particularly intriguing because of the historical circumstances surrounding it. Between 1861 and 1881, Angus McDonald, a one-time chief factor for the Hudson's Bay Company at Fort Colville, made a few trips from the Flathead country in Montana to Vancouver Island. On one of these journeys he mentioned meeting a tall, two-hundred-pound Indian who called himself Jamaiakan. Many years ago, the Indian claimed, he had climbed the mountain and fasted for five days and nights on its summit. The fast, a popular ritual, was the severest test of his entire life. His story suggests that the summit of Rainier might in fact have been conquered long before the first explorers and settlers arrived.

The earliest recorded discovery of Mount Rainier was an indirect consequence of the eighteenth-century maritime rivalry in the North Pacific. The race for sea otter skins brought both European and American ships to the Washington coast. Consequently, in May of 1792, Captain George Vancouver of the Royal British Navy sailed his sloop of war,

Rainier National Park Company brochure, circa 1925. *Courtesy Special Collections, University of Washington Libraries.*

Nature's Cathedral

SINCE dawn of history, men have worshipped Mountains. Those towering sentinels hurled heavenward by some giant manservant of Mother Nature in ages long forgot, have played, down through the ages, their silent part in the spiritual uplift of mankind.

Always have men groped for things above. As giant beacons of the face of mother earth, have Mountains served to call men always up and on. In reverent awe have men beheld their Mountains and always will so long as there exists the age-old scheme of life.

And so do we, of this new age, pay silent tribute to that heritage of ours from on down through the centuries; the love of mighty Mountains. Not as our ancient forbears, whose simple pagan minds saw them as living, ruling powers or royal abodes of reigning lords, omnipotent; but rather, we who see them find in these mighty peaks a new awakened interest in the life that is about us. Living, striving, winning, are the better for their influence.

Willard Cox

Discovery, into Puget Sound. Heading southward, he carefully recorded his impressions of this unexplored inland sea and its surrounding topography. As he scanned the mountain range filling the eastern horizon, he noted a "round snowy mountain" dominating the scene. He named it "Mount Rainier" in honor of his friend Rear Admiral Peter Rainier. Although Vancouver sailed far down Puget Sound, he commented that Rainier's "elevated summit was yet at a very considerable distance from shore." Apparently neither Vancouver nor any member of his crew attempted to reach the mountain by land, or for that matter even considered the idea. That honor would go to another Englishman, Dr. William Fraser Tolmie, a physician for the Hudson's Bay Company.

Tolmie arrived at the company's newly constructed post, Fort Nisqually, in 1833. His botanical interests soon attracted him to Mount Rainier, where he hoped to gather herbs for medicines. Indians familiar with the mountains apparently told him which areas offered the best chances for success, so his party of six, including himself, an Indian guide, and four other natives, made the trip in late summer. The men followed the Puyallup River to its junction with the Mowich River, and then past Mowich Lake into the northwest section of the present park. Although Tolmie may not have actually climbed the crest now bearing his name, Tolmie Peak, he was the first explorer on record to venture within the present confines of the national park.

Not long after Tolmie's historic trip, Americans began to settle on farms in the Willamette Valley of Oregon and at Indian missions east of the Cascades. Added American interest in West Coast harbors prompted President Martin Van Buren to implement a long-planned naval expedition to the Pacific Ocean, including Puget Sound. This extraordinary voyage (1838–41) was commanded by Lieutenant Charles Wilkes, a bright and highly capable officer skilled in marine mapping. Officially known as the United States Exploring Expedition, its scientists were extremely thorough. From the Antarctic to Puget Sound, Wilkes and his associates mapped coastal waters, noted Indian linguistics, studied harbors and inlets, and collected numerous specimens. One of the overland expeditions, led by Lieutenant Robert E. Johnson, made the round trip between Fort Nisqually and Fort Colville over Naches Pass, the old Indian Trail connecting eastern and western Washington. An important result was the first known study of the elevation of Mount Rainier. Thus did Johnson's venture transcend curiosity about the mountain and presage the era of scientific investigation in the American West.

In the wake of the explorers, thousands of emigrant settlers risked life and property on the long and arduous journey to the Pacific Northwest via the Oregon Trail. Among the argonauts of the 1840s and the 1850s was James Longmire, an intrepid pioneer destined to leave his mark on the early history of Mount Rainier National Park. With his family and associates, he helped lead an epic crossing of Naches Pass in 1853, the first crossing of its kind over the Cascades north of the Columbia River.

The attraction for Longmire was free land in the newly created Washington Territory. After leaving Shawnee Prairie, Indiana, the Longmire wagon train arrived on the Naches River in eastern Washington late in the summer of 1853. The wagon train crossed and recrossed the river sixty-eight times, and on the west side of Naches Pass, the men had to lower the wagons inch by inch down the precipitous slopes. Finally, seven months after leaving Indiana, the pioneers reached the Nisqually Plains south of the present city of Tacoma. While others took up land claims along Puget Sound, James Longmire crossed the Nisqually River and claimed 640 acres on Yelm Prairie, the base for his many summer trips to Mount Rainier in years to come.

Most "mountain talk" in the 1850s was not about recreation; instead, residents of Puget Sound were concerned about improving Naches Pass, or finding a better east-west route through the Cascades. Toward that end, James Longmire and William Packwood searched for a new route south of Mount Rainier. Their decision in 1854 to follow the Nisqually River system on the southwest side of the mountain was significant, for once again, more than twenty years after Tolmie's approach from the northwest, curiosity drew men close to the massive peak.

Longmire's and Packwood's efforts led to the discovery of Cowlitz Pass, though it never developed into a main route of travel. One important reason was the growing tendency among incoming settlers to set out for the Puget Sound country from Portland, avoiding the Cascade Mountains altogether.

Longmire's preoccupation with his Yelm Prairie homestead and service during the Indian wars of 1855–58 prevented him from returning to Mount Rainier until 1861. In the meantime, Lieutenant A. V. Kautz, an army officer from Fort Steilacoom, made a daring attempt on Rainier's summit in 1857. With a support team of four soldiers, a medical doctor, and an Indian guide, Kautz and one of the soldiers struggled up the rugged south slope between Nisqually and Kautz glaciers, managing to climb within a few hundred feet of the top before turning back. He made no plans for a second assault on the peak, nor did he think it likely that anyone else would try in the immediate future. He accurately predicted, however, that civilization would bring many changes, and eventually a successful ascent. "When the locomotive is heard in that region some day," he observed, and "American enterprise has established an ice cream saloon at the foot of the glacier, attempts to ascend that magnificent snow-peak will be quite different." Meanwhile, he concluded, "many a long year will pass away before roads are sufficiently good enough to induce anyone to do what we did in the summer of 1857."

James Longmire in particular preferred to explore the environs at Mount Rainier rather than its slopes. In 1861 he blazed a packhorse trail between his Yelm Prairie homestead and Bear Prairie, near the southwest corner of the present park. Subsequently, he began extensive explorations of the mountain's base. In time, as his reputation for discovery increased, early climbers anxiously sought his advice regarding the best approaches to the higher slopes. Increasingly, Longmire guided climbers and others through the foothills, and ultimately played an important role in the first successful ascent of the summit in 1870.

In August of that year, a three-man climbing team from Olympia persuaded Longmire to lead the way to Bear Prairie in the first stage of an attempt to conquer the peak. The climbers—General Hazard Stevens, Philomen Van Trump, and Edward T. Coleman—were, in turn, guided by Sluiskin, a Yakima Indian, on a long and circuitous route over the Tatoosh Range, up Mazama Ridge, and finally to a waterfall—named Sluiskin Falls by Stevens and Van Trump—at the upper end of what would become known as Paradise Valley. At that point, Sluiskin refused to go any farther, warning Stevens and Van Trump (Coleman had already given up and returned to camp) to abandon what he believed was a very foolish and fateful venture.

According to Stevens, Sluiskin believed the men would die if they continued on, for "Takhoma" was an "enchanted" mountain inhabited by an evil spirit who dwelt in a fiery lake on its summit. When Sluiskin realized his words were to no avail, he told the climbers he would wait for them for three days, and if they failed to return, he would go to Olympia to inform their friends of their deaths. It was a promise he did not have to fulfill. Stevens and Van Trump successfully struggled to the top of Mount Rainier up its southwest flank, then descended without mishap. They returned to Olympia to a rousing welcome, for they had accomplished what many had thought to be the impossible.

The second ascent of Rainier was not far distant. Late in that same summer of 1870, James Longmire once again served as guide. This time S. F. Emmons and A. D. Wilson successfully made the assault via a variation of the Stevens–Van Trump route. Emmons was especially intrigued by the nature of the Nisqually, Cowlitz, and White (now Emmons) glaciers. He also described in some detail the three peaks that form the summit of the mountain, noting that the one to the east, known today as Columbia Crest, was the highest. His most memorable sight, however, was White Glacier, the largest single glacier in the United States outside of Alaska.

Fully thirteen years elapsed before the third successful ascent of Mount Rainier. Van Trump, back for a second time with a new associate, George Bayley, even persuaded James Longmire (at age 63) to join them in going all the way to the summit in Aug-

Climbers in crevasse area on Nisqually
Glacier, n.d. *Photo by Asahel Curtis.*
Courtesy University of Washington.

ust of 1883. Indian Henry, who was as familiar with the Mount Rainier area as Longmire, accompanied them to Paradise Valley, where the climbers left him and followed the same route taken by the two previous parties in 1870. Unlike the earlier ascents, however, this party decided to stay overnight on the summit, where steam vents provided a somewhat warm but discomforting night's rest. When the climbers returned to their base camp on the Nisqually River, James Longmire discovered bubbling mineral springs in a meadow where his pack horses had strayed.

Following up on his good fortune, Longmire filed a mineral claim under the Federal Placer Act on the area around the springs. Next, he built a spur trail to his claim from Bear Prairie and began to construct a crude tourist resort, laying the foundation to Longmire Springs, or Longmire's Medical Springs. The enterprise eventually attracted thousands of people, who in turn told others about the region.

The northwest side of the mountain, known as the Carbon River area, also loomed as a potentially great tourist attraction. As early as the 1880s, railroad and mining interests had surveyed and built trails into that wilderness; notable in this regard was the work of Bailey T. Willis, an assistant geologist for the Northern Transcontinental Survey.

Willis's enthusiasm for the Carbon River area soon aroused the curiosity of Thomas F. Oakes,

vice president of the Northern Pacific Railway, who decided to visit the area himself to verify Willis's glowing account. Accordingly, in June of 1883, a contingent including Oakes, Senator George Edmunds of Vermont, and J.M. Buckley, assistant general manager of the Northern Pacific in charge of western divisions, explored this rugged and remote flank of Rainier. Oakes returned from the trip thoroughly convinced that the area did indeed have great potential for tourism. Furthermore, Oakes predicted the Northern Pacific Railway would play a key role in realizing that potential. "A very important part of the business of a railroad company is to provide incentives for travel," he noted, pointing to company promotion of the "great National Yellowstone Park." Now, he promised, the same advertising and publicity would be invested in Mount Rainier, or Mount Tacoma as the railroad officially decided to call the mountain in 1883.

By 1883 the era of discovery and exploration had drawn to a close, but by no means had such activities ceased. The entire east side of Rainier was still largely unexplored, and mountain climbers themselves were just beginning to find new routes to the summit. But the discovery of Longmire Springs and the opening of the Carbon River country ushered in a new era, that of tourism. Publicity about Mount Rainier was on the rise and provided the momentum that would lead to national park protection in 1899.

The Tacoma Hotel. Opened in 1884, "The Tacoma" was widely known as a popular tourist stop. Built on a bluff overlooking Puget Sound, it offered a commanding view of Mount Rainier. The hotel was destroyed by fire in 1935. *Courtesy Washington State Historical Society.*

PLEASURE SEEKERS AND PRESERVATIONISTS

The cabin underway at Longmire Springs during the summer of 1884 would have appeared tiny if placed side by side with the great hotel rising at the same time in Tacoma. The cabin was designed and built by James Longmire; the hotel, by the famous New York architect Stanford White. Seattle and Portland marveled as the Northern Pacific Railway poured $267,000 into the sprawling building; Longmire also took pride in his own structure, the first permanent building within what would later become national park boundaries. No one fully realized it then, but the Tacoma Hotel and Longmire's cabin helped usher in the age of tourism in northwest Washington State. Longmire followed his cabin with a small log inn to serve the few venturesome travelers coming to the mountain. Meanwhile, The Tacoma, which gained a national reputation in a remarkably short time, was also instrumental in attracting tourists to both Mount Rainier and the Puget Sound country.

The grand hotel in Tacoma was especially symbolic of the boom time that stirred the Pacific Northwest beginning in the 1880s. For the next three decades, largely stimulated by the arrival of the northern transcontinental railroads between 1883 and 1893, the region experienced unprecedented change and rapid population growth. Seattle alone jumped from a population of only 3,500 in 1880 to more than 237,000 in 1910, while Tacoma surged from 1,000 to more than 100,000. As the cities rose,

Longmire Springs Hotel, operated by the James Longmire family until 1915. June 29, 1912. *Photo by Curtis and Miller. Courtesy Washington State Historical Society.*

and their surrounding forests were felled, people throughout the region confidently predicted ever greater things for the future.

It followed that tourism might also flourish in the region. The city of Tacoma, already in a race with Seattle and Portland to become the region's leading city, thus made every effort to capitalize on its proximity to Mount Rainier. The "City of Destiny," as its promoters fondly described it, lay at the very doorstep to the mountain. Tacoma was indeed the only "natural" departure for tourists en route to Longmire Springs, Paradise Valley, or the Carbon River area.

Built of brick and stone, the Tacoma Hotel rested on a bluff one hundred feet above Puget Sound. Here guests enjoyed a panoramic view of the lowlands and mountains, especially Mount Rainier. One's stay at the hotel was accented by an atmosphere of luxurious rooms, fine dining, orchestra music in the parlor, and service with a flourish. For the growing number of guests eager to visit Mount Rainier, the hotel further specialized in guided mountain travel. Of course, the overwhelming number of tourists had no interest in scaling the mountain, but rather in catching a grand view from lower elevations, or getting just close enough to examine a glacier. Eventually, guests traveled to Longmire Springs and Paradise Valley; initially, however, the Tacoma Hotel signed up most people for trips over the Cascade division of the Northern

The Guide Service, circa 1927, was operated by the Rainier National Park Company. The guides pictured above led tourists to glaciers and the summit, the latter a long, arduous trek. *Courtesy Special Collections, University of Washington Libraries.*

Packtrain at Klapatche Lake, September 10, 1918. *Photo by Asahel Curtis. Courtesy Washington State Historical Society.*

Pacific Railway from Tacoma to Wilkeson, the entrance to the Carbon River country. At Wilkeson tourists hired horses and guides for the remainder of the trip.

The round trip from Tacoma to the Carbon River high country, requiring five or six days, cost about sixty dollars per person, or fifty dollars per person in a party of two or more. Guides, such as George Driver, proprietor of the Valley Hotel in Wilkeson, soon earned reputations throughout the region. Most guides, of course, promoted their reputations simply by warning those attracted to the rugged slopes never to venture into that "wild country" alone.

For wild country, it was indeed spectacular. Consequently, as early as 1883, Karl von Zittel of Germany and James Bryce of England strongly urged the United States government to enclose Mount

Mount Rainier from Lake Washington, 1903. *Photo by Asahel Curtis. Courtesy Washington State Historical Society.*

Rainier in a national park. The Carbon River country especially impressed Zittel and Bryce as unique in the world for natural beauty. They marveled, for example, at the tremendous ice formations of the Carbon and Mowich glaciers, both jaggedly crevassed and thousands of feet—even miles—in length. The region reminded them of Norway, with its combination of huge stands of timber, imposing glaciers, and swift rivers, yet the awesome heights of Mount Rainier overshadowed even their fondest memories. In a letter to congressional leaders, Zittel and Bryce therefore expressed the hope that Mount Rainier, "like Yosemite Valley and Yellowstone, be reserved by the federal government and treated as a national park." Accordingly, they were the first on record to urge the creation of Mount Rainier National Park, although many other visitors were also hoping for the same result.

While increasing numbers of tourists and travelers marveled at the Carbon River country, James Longmire and his family bustled about their mineral springs developing a health spa. Still, it was no simple task splitting cedar to put up buildings, nor digging out springs and fitting them with cedar tubs. Similarly, furniture had to be fashioned by hand for the many tourists expected to arrive.

Meanwhile, there remained the problem of assuring adequate transportation to the springs. A comfortable resort would be pointless if people still could not reach it. Every spring, the trail from the Northern Pacific's Yelm Station had to be cleared of new obstacles so that horses, carrying both supplies and tourists from Olympia, could get through as quickly as possible. For the greater numbers of tourists who came from Tacoma, James Longmire solicited help to open the old trail from Eatonville up the Nisqually River. In 1884, with the aid of some Indians, the Longmire "road gang" built a wagon road between Succotash Valley (Ashford) and the springs, a distance of thirteen miles. Others worked on the new road to Eatonville, thus making it possible by 1891 for visitors to travel the sixty miles from Tacoma to Longmire Springs by wagon. Although the trips were rough and tiring by either route, most tourists considered any inconvenience worth the effort.

The mineral baths proved especially popular. A good soaking in the "health-giving waters" not only cured common ailments, but restored one's vigor and appearance. Of course, Mount Rainier was a summer attraction; when snow began to fall, the Longmires closed the hotel and returned to Yelm Prairie until the following April or May.

In addition to operating their resort, the Longmires actively explored the region, constructing trails and bestowing place names throughout much of the present park. In 1885 Elcaine Longmire's wife, Martha, named Paradise Valley, now the most famous of all Mount Rainier sites. In 1895 James Longmire and his son Elcaine with grandsons Leonard and Ben, finally completed the construction of the first trail from Longmire Springs to the valley.

Just how many other place names can be attributed to the Longmires is unknown, but they were numerous. Ben Longmire alone probably originated more place names than any other person in the history of the park. A bachelor, whose only "loves" seem to have been his mules and the woods, he named Fisher's Hornpipe Creek, Devil's Dream Canyon (and creek), Ipsut Pass, Mowich Lake, and Martha Falls, to mention only a few. In his typical,

Stages in front of National Park Inn at Longmire Springs, June 1911. The inn opened on July 1, 1906, and was operated by the Tacoma Eastern Railroad, a subsidiary of the Chicago, Milwaukee, St. Paul, and Pacific Railway. The inn was destroyed by fire in 1926. *Photo by Asahel Curtis. Courtesy Washington State Historical Society.*

Hikers on Mount Ararat looking at Mount Rainier, August 20, 1913. *Photo by Asahel Curtis. Courtesy Washington State Historical Society.*

colorful way, he further noted that he named Mount Ararat "because I found there some long slabs of wood that had turned to stone, and I thought they might have been part of old Noah's boat."

Another example of Ben's novel place-naming style is Ipsut Pass, which he and Bill Stafford named in 1914. They were laying out the Wonderland Trail section in the Carbon River area, when Ben asked Stafford to scout for a passage from Carbon River up over the steep ridge to Mowich Lake. Upon completing his survey, Stafford informed Ben he had indeed "found a narrow pass, but, gee, it's up!" Somehow, through the years, the original place name of Itsup Pass became distorted, leading to the present spelling, Ipsut Pass.

The Longmire name is also associated, indirectly, with the old silver forest burn still in evidence on the road to Paradise Valley near Narada Falls. In

September of 1894, James Longmire and Phil Kelly were returning to the springs with pack horses from Paradise Valley, when the horses encountered yellow jackets. They were stung several times, and one of the frightened animals, in a state of frenzy, jumped into the river and nearly drowned. After considerable difficulty, the two men managed to calm the horses and continue down the trail. When they reached the springs, they decided to return to the spot where the bees were and burn out the pests before other hikers and horses got the same treatment. The fire did the job, but Longmire and Kelly never figured that the flames would get out of hand. Wind blowing against the ridge, coupled with the fire's own draft, swept it out of control and up over the crest. The sizable area burned showed the scars of hundreds of scorched trees. In time these trees turned silver-gray, and thus became known as the silver forest. More than twenty years after the fire, logs cut out of this area became part of Paradise Inn.

Unquestionably, the Longmire family's varied mountain life substantially accelerated public awareness of the Mount Rainier region. But perhaps the climbers, including a few Longmires, generated the most news and interest. For two decades following the discovery of Longmire Springs, those who succeeded in climbing the mountain, and even some who did not, continued to make front-page news. They strongly shared a common experience, one that not only helped spread the fame of Mount Rain-

Party in crevasse, Nisqually Glacier, 1917. *Photo by Asahel Curtis. Courtesy Washington State Historical Society.*

ier, but also inspired concern for preserving it in its natural setting.

Prominent people lent further support to the preservation idea by coming long distances to climb Mount Rainier. In 1888, for example, John Muir, famous for his own fight to protect Yosemite Valley, climbed the peak. Muir, of course, strongly advocated national park status for the area.

The summit party of Leonard (Len) Longmire's in August 1890 also attracted great attention. Included in his party was Fay Fuller of Tacoma, the first woman to reach the top of Rainier. Fuller expressed the thrill of her memorable experience in "A Trip to the Summit," published in *Every Sunday,* a Tacoma newspaper, on August 23, 1890.

In 1891 two more women, Edith Corbett and Susy Longmire, reached the summit. Although still fewer than forty people could say they had conquered it, fascination with the sport of mountaineering grew rapidly. In turn, as more and more people traveled to Rainier, the demand for improved transportation between the mountain and Puget Sound communities grew proportionately. So, too, did calls for the establishment of additional accommodations at Paradise Valley. To be sure, by the mid-1890s, a few enterprising individuals recognized that hotel services in the scenic alpine valley would be a good investment. "Charlie" Comstock of nearby Elbe, Washington, pioneered the business in the summer of 1895 with a makeshift coffe shop

called Paradise Hotel. Later, from 1898 to 1915, John Reese operated a tent lodging business, with meals, on the slopes of the valley. He called his rustic accommodations, Camp of the Clouds, although visitors obviously received more than just a spot to throw down a bedroll.

Meanwhile, local businessmen actively promoted better roads and transportation services to Longmire Springs. These entrepreneurs, of course, were fully aware that more tourists simply added up to more patronage for their establishments. Still, aside from exerting pressure to make Mount Rainier more accessible, the local business community contributed significantly to the national park movement. Business leaders poured thousands of dollars into large-scale promotional campaigns, advertising the mountain as one of the nation's outstanding natural playgrounds.

The western railroads were especially active along these lines. On July 14, 1890, for example, the Milwaukee Road incorporated the Tacoma Eastern Railroad Company. Its tracks were to run south and east to tap lumber, mineral, and agricultural resources between Tacoma and the Cascades. In addition, passenger service to Mount Rainier seemed a distinct and lucrative possibility. The depression of 1893, unfortunately, suspended the project. Work finally resumed in 1900, and by 1904 the Tacoma Eastern reached as far as Ashford, seven miles outside the present southwestern boundary of the park.

Reese's Camp of the Clouds below Alta Vista, upper Paradise Valley, 1910. *Photo by Asahel Curtis. Courtesy Washington State Historical Society.*

Tacoma Eastern Railroad logo, circa 1911. *Courtesy University of Washington.*

In the interim, horse-drawn stages still carried most of the tourists between Tacoma and Longmire Springs.

The typical itinerary of a traveler to Rainier in the 1890s began with a night at the Tacoma Hotel, where the visitor probably thumbed through a copy of Fred G. Plummer's *Illustrated Guide to Mount Tacoma.* The back cover included a picture of the Tacoma Hotel and a statement reading: "Headquarters for Tourists, Commercial Men, and Climbers of Mount Tacoma—Full equipment and guides for Mountain climbing on one day's notice." Here the traveler also learned about the dozen livery stables in Tacoma, the Jefferson Avenue electric car, and the local railroad, any of which provided transportation to Lake Park (Spanaway), a distance of approximately thirteen miles from the city. Stages departed from Lake Park for the mountain every morning at nine o'clock sharp. After an overnight stop in Eatonville, the stage continued to Longmire Springs. In 1896 the Tacoma Carriage and Baggage Transfer Company started direct stage service between Tacoma and Longmire Springs on a semi-weekly basis; the roundtrip cost was eight dollars.

These developments in transportation services had a promotional spinoff for the park movement. In the late 1890s even the early bicycle enthusiasts, known as Wheelmen, exerted considerable pressure on the county and the new state government to improve the road to Mount Rainier. The simple truth was that growing numbers of tourists, mostly from local communities, had discovered Rainier, and now wanted the way to its slopes cleared and improved as quickly as possible.

The Tacoma Hotel, circa 1918. *Photo by M. D. Boland. Courtesy Washington State Historical Society.*

THE
NATIONAL PARK
CAMPAIGN

By the 1890s, citizens and preservationists nationwide questioned whether or not Mount Rainier would fall victim to commercial exploitation. True, the movement calling for the creation of a national park seemed to have widespread support locally from both commercial and preservation interests. But the latter could never be sure about the former's ulterior motives. Support from the business community was desirable, even necessary, since the development of roads and hotel services required money and publicity. Yet no preservationist could take comfort in the thought that

a national park enclosing Mount Rainier might turn into a resort rather than a sanctuary for plants and wildlife. Furthermore, until Congress actually created the park, little prevented logging interests, grazers, and miners from invading the proposed national park itself. In fact, the actions of careless campers in Paradise Valley during the 1890s (chopping trees, leaving messy campsites, and abusing wildlife) was enough to sound the alarm.

Enthusiastic and active promoters of protection for Mount Rainier—Bailey Willis, Cyrus Mosier, Fred G. Plummer, P. B. Van Trump, E. C. Smith, E. T. Allen, and others—found national support from the National Geographical Society, the Geological Society, the American Association for the

Klapatche Lake on west side, 1910. *Photo by Asahel Curtis. Courtesy Washington State Historical Society.*

29

Advancement of Science, and the Appalachian and Sierra mountain clubs. Local organizations, such as the Washington Alpine Club (formed in 1893), were further encouraged by growing awareness about conservation among the American people at large. Yellowstone National Park, Wyoming, had been created as early as 1872, and in 1890 Congress established three more parks in California: Yosemite, Sequoia, and General Grant. Mount Rainier would be the fifth national park. As preservationists soon discovered, however, it was one thing to arouse public opinion, but quite another to make the national park a reality. Rainier boosters were painfully aware of legislative inertia, and knew that the federal government would have to be convinced to protect Mount Rainier in perpetuity.

Fortunately for the Rainier park movement, Cyrus A. Mosier, special agent for the Interior Department, came west in 1891 to investigate timber conditions surrounding Mount Rainier as a preliminary step to the possible establishment of forest reservations. His assignment was, in part, a direct consequence of the Act of 1891, a milestone in the history of forest legislation. The act authorized the creation of forest reservations (later known as national forests), and thus served as the basis for the establishment in 1905 of the United States Forest Service. Since much of the public domain in the Pacific Northwest included huge tracts of valuable timber, Mosier's investigation was of high priority.

On this particular outing, he focused on Mount Rainier and its environs. To his alarm, he noted that dangers associated with timber destruction were terribly real. If speculators in particular were not restrained, he predicted catastrophic results for the high country and lowlands, including floods, erosion, pollution, fire, and scarring of the natural beauty. Indeed, the speculation, he remarked, intended to "strip the base" of Mount Rainier of its timber, tearing "the frame from this grand painting against the sky." Nor would they be satisfied, he warned, "till every tree is felled or burned and the face of the country laid waste." Land laws supposedly intended to aid settlers provided loopholes through which corporations had "stealthily crept into possession and acquired title to a large part of the most valuable redwood, pine, fir, and cedar lands on the Pacific Coast."

Mosier also sharply criticized the campers in Paradise Valley, who thoughtlessly defaced trees or intentionally set fires to the magnificent groves just to see the trees ablaze. Similarly, he urged the federal government to put a stop to the Indian practice of setting fires in lightly timbered areas of the Cascade Range to increase the berry crop from year to year. Likewise, grazing interests often fired the timber to increase the spread of grasses, a practice Mosier equally condemned.

Although the impact of Mosier's report cannot be measured fully, on February 20, 1893, President

Secretary of the Interior Franklin K. Lane (fourth from left) and party posing in front of Mount Rainier and the Nisqually Glacier, August 16, 1913. *Photo by Asahel Curtis. Courtesy Washington State Historical Society.*

Benjamin Harrison proclaimed the establishment of the Pacific Forest Reserve. The forest reservation ran the length of the mountain range through west central Washington, including present Mount Rainier National Park. Soon afterward, President Grover Cleveland changed the title to Mount Rainier Forest Reserve, and a few years later, the federal lands surrounding Rainier park were designated the Mount Rainier National Forest. For the moment, the establishment of the Pacific Forest Reserve in 1893 was a decisive turning point for park enthusiasts; as government property, the forest lands encompassing Mount Rainier could easily be redesignated a national park.

Bolstered by endorsements from scientific and conservation societies around the country, Rainier enthusiasts called for a national park in resolutions, petitions, and newspaper articles. As early as December 23, 1893, for example, Senator Watson C. Squire of Washington State presented Congress a petition from the Seattle Chamber of Commerce, requesting the establishment of Washington National Park. The major obstacle to congressional approval was the commissioner of public lands, who persuaded Secretary of the Interior Hoke Smith to oppose the bill in its original form. The commissioner did not accept the boundaries as proposed, because too much land seemed to be included. Besides, the commissioner argued, the federal government had already provided for appropriate protection and use of the area as forest reservations.

In addition, money for administration of the park would have to be authorized by Congress. Opponents further argued that hundreds of other beautiful areas in the United States were not national parks, while still other critics questioned whether or not scenic wonders such as Mount Rainier might not be better administered under state rather than federal jurisdiction. These and similar questions were raised many times during the 1890s while Washington State's delegation fought to get the park bill enacted.

Still, progress had been made. Coupled with the creation of the Pacific Forest Reserve, Senator Squire's work in 1893 was of paramount importance. Moreover, by 1896 the negativism of the General Land Office had been largely offset by the report of the Forest Commission. Its strong endorsement of forest protection, was the direct outcome of concern among a few influential easterners regarding destruction of the nation's forest lands. The group included Charles S. Sargent, editor of *Garden and Forest;* Alexander Agassiz, curator of the Harvard Museum of Comparative Zoology; Gifford Pinchot, a young professional forester; Arnold Hague of the U.S. Geological Survey; Carl Schurz, former interior secretary under President Rutherford B. Hayes; Robert Underwood Johnson, editor of *Century Magazine;* and Dr. Walcott Gibbs, head of the National Academy of Sciences.

Among the chief concerns of the Forest Commission was the future of the public domain, specifically, how to apply sound management to its dwindling stands of commercial timber. Above all, the commission called for the curtailment of reckless exploitation and the protection of major watersheds. Accordingly, as the commissioners toured the West in the summer of 1896, they recommended the creation of more forest reservations, including three in Washington State alone. Their report also urged the creation of two national parks, Grand Canyon and Mount Rainier. In this manner, new life was pumped into the Rainier park movement.

The revival had come none too soon. In 1897 President Grover Cleveland suddenly designated thirteen new forest reservations by presidential proclamation. In Washington State, the Washington, Olympic, and Mount Rainier forest reserves closed about six million acres to further private use. Especially among grazing interests, Cleveland's proclamations were simply unacceptable; they preferred the old system of prohibitions but no enforcement. With the creation of the new reserves, the grazers feared enforcement in the forests was finally at hand.

In retrospect, however, the grazers made more noise than opposition to the park movement. The same could be said of mining interests, a few of whom dabbled within the present park area. Like the grazers, they found lands at lower elevations were actually more promising. Nonetheless, supporters of the Rainier park movement feared the possibility of miners desecrating the landscape. During the 1880s and 1890s, miners and mining companies were staking claims throughout the Cascades. On the outskirts of Mount Rainier, in places such as Eatonville, Wilkeson, Carbonado, Crystal Mountain, Gold Hill, Summit Creek, and upper White River, miners failed to locate significant amounts of silver and copper. In their disappointment, they hoped to make the "big strike" elsewhere; accordingly, they wished to protect their options for exploiting the slopes of Mount Rainier. Fortunately, mining within the proposed park also proved unrewarding, and, ultimately, the miners' opposition to the park movement was therefore only a nuisance.

Railroad lands within the proposed park were a more serious complication. In its original charter of 1864, the Northern Pacific Railway received title to every other square mile of federal property within twenty miles on either side of its right-of-way. Officials within the Interior Department advised Congress not to establish the park until these railroad claims had been exchanged for other federal lands.

The railroad issue stalled the Washington National Park bill long enough to prevent final enactment in 1897. The bill passed both houses of Congress only to arrive at the president's desk too late in the session for his signature. Rainier supporters tried again in 1898 and 1899. By that time the bill had been rewritten to grant the Northern Pacific lieu land rights in exchange for relinquishing its lands on Mount Rainier.

Preservationists faced yet another hurdle in the opposition of Congressman "Uncle Joe" Cannon of Illinois. As chief lieutenant to Thomas Reed, Speaker of the House, Cannon had great authority. He argued that supporters of the park would come back to Congress time and again to ask for money. The "place isn't worth it," he remarked, "and we don't want to throw our money away." Senator John Wilson and Representative James Lewis of Washington, accompanied by John P. Hartman, another leading figure in the park movement, met Cannon to hammer out a compromise. The trio promised Cannon not to request appropriations for the park as long as he was a member of Congress. Although the compromise was hard to swallow, and indeed was to haunt Mount Rainier development for several years, at long last the proposed Washington National Park would be created.

In the last moments, Congressman John F. Lacey of Iowa, chairman of the House Committee on Public lands, successfully amended the bill to read "Mount Rainier National Park." Knowledge of this eleventh hour amendment apparently did not reach Washington State until after President William McKinley signed the bill on March 2, 1899. When the news broke, long-standing resentment against use of the name Rainier resurfaced in Tacoma. It is not clear whether the city wanted the park called Mount Tacoma National Park or Washington National Park, with the peak in the latter case known officially as Mount Tacoma. Definitely, however, Tacomans did not want the name Rainier applied either to the mountain or to the park. Ever since the Northern Pacific Railway entered Tacoma in 1883, railroad officials and city residents had strongly objected to Rainier as a foreign term. Tacoma, they concluded, was the appropriate designation, both for their city and the mountain.

Still, creation of the park in the first place was of greatest importance. As yet, only a few Americans subscribed to the conviction that certain areas of the public domain ought to be protected for their scenic beauty. Certainly, the participants of the Mount Rainier park movement had contributed significantly to that ideal.

THE ROAD TO PARADISE

The establishment of Mount Rainier National Park in 1899 pleased preservationists and developers alike. All agreed that basic developments—road access, backcountry trails, public services, and resource protection—were necessary for this great scenic attraction. In time, as occurred in other national parks, early allies would part company over issues of public use, but during the park's first years, Rainier's supporters wanted the same things. A few disgruntled miners, grazers, and hunters were exceptions, but none of these groups

Two auto stages at Nisqually Entrance, June 29, 1912. *Photo by Asahel Curtis. Courtesy Washington State Historical Society.*

proved a major threat to the new park.

Rainier, like the four previous national parks, still passed through a period of administrative uncertainty. Congress authorized the Interior Department to formulate rules and regulations for Mount Rainier, but Secretary Ethan Allen Hitchcock and his field staffs were given no special appropriations for administration and development of the new park. Not until 1902 did some semblance of organized protection and management emerge when Hitchcock temporarily placed G. F. Allen, supervisor of the Mount Rainier Forest Reserve, in charge of the park as well. Beginning with the help of two seasonal rangers in 1903 and a budget of a few hundred dollars (excluding road project mon-

Near park boundary on Naches Pass Highway, July 20, 1919. *Photo by Asahel Curtis. Courtesy Washington State Historical Society.*

ey), Allen managed Mount Rainier National Park on a part-time basis through 1909. In that period he introduced basic game and fire protection, supervised the construction and maintenance of trails, expanded the staff to include two permanent and four seasonal rangers, and successfully urged the repeal in 1908 of the mining clause in the park act.

During the first years of park development, the Longmire Springs–Paradise Valley area required practically all of the government's administrative and financial attention. Between 1899 and 1903, about 2,000 people traveled to this popular section of the park, and by 1906 nearly that many visitors came in a single season. In 1911 more than 10,000 people and probably 1,100 cars and auto stages entered the park at the Nisqually Entrance below Longmire Springs. In contrast, throughout 1911 only 400 or so visitors went to the Carbon River country on the northwestern side of the park; in fact, so few travelers trekked over to the eastern side, that park records do not officially list a number until 1912, when a mere 175 people came over the Ohanapecosh Trail. Clearly, the pattern of tourist travel to the park had been set: most people went to Paradise Valley.

Access by the only road leading to the park—and tourist accommodations along the route—explain the popularity of the Longmire-Paradise area. The road at the turn of the century was known locally as the Mountain Road. Its condition varied greatly, especially over the last thirteen miles, where

One-way traffic on the road to Paradise, 1917. *Photo by Asahel Curtis. Courtesy Washington State Historical Society.*

travelers suffered through deep ruts and teeth-jarring potholes. From Longmire Springs tourists rode horses to their final destination in Paradise Valley. Such primitive conditions today may hold a certain romantic appeal, but when they were commonplace, people demanded the standard improvements. Accordingly, as the number of automobiles and touring buses increased, so did the construction of roads.

In the case of Mount Rainier, public pressure for good roads can be linked to the park's proximity to Tacoma and Seattle. Congressmen from the state of Washinton carried the concerns of urban recreationists to the nation's capital, where Congress in 1903 approved an appropriation of $10,000 to survey a road in the park. Although no specific location of the road was predetermined, it would be somewhere between Longmire Springs and Paradise Valley. The secretary of war appointed Major Hiram M. Chittenden of the Army Corps of Engineers to supervise the survey from his Seattle office. Chittenden delegated the actual work in the field to Eugene Ricksecker, his assistant engineer in Tacoma.

Compared to the challenge that lay above the springs, widening and reinforcing the base of the old wagon road that ended at Longmire gave Ricksecker little to worry about. Beyond the springs the road would rise almost 3,000 feet to its end at Paradise. The grade could not be more than four per cent if automobiles and other self-powered vehicles were to negotiate the climb. For vehicles to pass safely, the width of the road had to be from sixteen to eighteen feet. Curves and switchbacks compounded the problem. A great deal of rock would have to be removed, some places to a depth of eight feet, to assure a solid base. Similarly, bridges across glacier-fed streams had to withstand heavy traffic, winter freezing, and occasional flooding. Finally, it was important that the road be constructed to take advantage of the many scenic features along the way, such as mountain viewpoints, waterfalls, and canyons. Although the distance between the springs and Paradise was only thirteen miles, construction of the road required not only first-rate engineering but a good deal of patience.

In the spring of 1904 Congress granted an additional $30,000 for the road, awarding the project to a private contractor. Later, however, the government cancelled the agreement for unsatisfactory work and placed Ricksecker in direct charge of construction. Despite inclement weather and some labor problems, Ricksecker's crews reached Paradise Valley in September 1910. By that time, park authorities had opened the road as far as the Nisqually River crossing, five miles above the springs. In 1911 the first automobile reached Paradise Valley; however, the entire distance did not open to the public until 1915, and then only to one-way traffic the last seven miles.

As construction of the road progressed, the rate of travel to the park sharply increased. To herald the coming boom in tourism, more than two hundred

Caravan of auto stages winding through trees below Longmire Springs, June 29, 1912. *Photo by Asahel Curtis. Courtesy Washington State Historical Society.*

Tacoma Eastern passenger train to Ashford, Washington, seven miles outside Nisqually Entrance to Mount Rainier National Park, circa 1912. *Photo by Asahel Curtis. Courtesy Washington State Historical Society.*

representatives of the Alpine, Appalachian, Mazama, and Sierra clubs rendezvoused at Paradise in July of 1905. Meanwhile, the Tacoma Eastern Railroad had pushed its tracks to Ashford, seven miles outside the Nisqually Entrance. The railroad leased a two-acre tract at Longmire Springs, where it built a large hotel, the National Park Inn, which opened to the public on July 1, 1906. With tents to accommodate periodic overflow, the two-and-one-half-story hotel could sleep 250 people, while the Longmire Hotel could accommodate only thirty guests. The growing number of well-to-do tourists pre-ferred the luxury of the National Park Inn, another sign of the changing times.

Tent hotels catering to the middle class, however, also grew rapidly in number during the next decade. At Indian Henry's Hunting Ground, a superb scenic area located about seven miles by trail from Longmire Springs, George Hall and his wife (formerly Sue Longmire) opened Wigwam Hotel. At Paradise, John Reese's Camp of the Clouds featured over sixty tents and meal service by 1911. Because of the high elevation (5,400 feet) and heavy snowfall every winter, Reese's operations were limited to July and August. Nevertheless, his popular "hotel" never suffered from lack of business. With rail connections to Ashford, and the building and improvement of roads both inside and outside the park, tourists could travel between Puget Sound cities and Paradise, stay overnight, and return to their points of departure in half the time required for the same trip just a decade earlier.

Outside the western boundary of the park, on the mountain road from Tacoma, the main tourist stops included the Depot, Mashell, and Show hotels near Eatonville; the Canyon View Hotel at La Grande; the old, well-known Tourist Hotel at Elbe; and Kernahan's, Mesler's, and the Alpine in the Ashford area. The existence of these early tourist facilities both increased travel to Mount Rainier and alleviated some of the pressure for hotel service within the park.

Tour group in front of National Park Inn at Longmire Springs. Rotary Club "Mt. Tacoma Trip," August 25–26, 1911. *Photo by R. R. Raymoth. Courtesy Washington State Historical Society.*

Rainier National Park Company auto stages on road to Paradise, just above Longmire, 1930. *Courtesy Special Collections, University of Washington Libraries.*

Such amenities were a reflection of Rainier's growing popularity. In turn, mounting public pressure for more and better services, including road improvements, forced the Interior Department to set new priorities for the park. Interior Secretary Walter Fisher was particularly concerned in 1911 about inadequate concessions. Each year the government issued permits for a variety of services, ranging from rented automobiles to photographic shops and ice cream stands. The hotels themselves, while meeting the needs of tourists, nevertheless did so haphazardly and unsystematically. Some were clean and attractive, others were not. Even the recent National Park Inn at Longmire Springs no longer was considered a first-class hotel. Prices and services varied from concession to concession; since most permits ran out after only one year, concessions operated at the lowest possible cost, thus perpetuating the problem

Guides and inn employees promoting photographic service at Paradise, circa 1928. *Courtesy Washington State Historical Society.*

of unsatisfactory services. In Rainier, as throughout the national park system, only the establishment of the National Park Service in 1916 led to organized steps to correct the problem.

In the meantime, the parks had to fend for themselves. E. S. Hall, as park superintendent between 1910 and 1912, made the best of the concessionaire setup in Rainier; the main problem still was finding enough money to make the park accessible. Every-

thing hinged on getting sufficient appropriations from Congress, a complicated and formidable task. One of the barriers to acquiring funds beyond operating costs was the limited knowledge of Mount Rainier National Park held by most congressmen in Washington, D.C. People living in the Pacific Northwest, especially around Puget Sound, found it hard to believe that Congress could be so uninformed about a park they assumed to be world famous. In either case, Yellowstone, Yosemite, and the newly created Glacier National Park in Montana seemed to be getting far more recognition in Congress than Mount Rainier.

In March of 1912, Seattle and Tacoma commercial organizations held meetings to discuss how both cities could assist the superintendent of Rainier park in winning larger appropriations for the reserve. The groups included the new Seattle Chamber of Commerce, Seattle Commercial Club, Rotary Club of Seattle, the Tacoma Commercial Club and Chamber of Commerce, and the Rotary Club of Tacoma. As Mount Rainier activists, the assemblage decided to form the Seattle-Tacoma Rainier National Park Committee. Asahel Curtis, a noted Pacific Northwest photographer, was chosen chairman; T. H. Martin, a Tacoma businessman, was elected secretary. R. A. Ballinger of Seattle, formerly interior secretary under President William Howard Taft, and A. H. Denman, of Tacoma, were two other prominent persons in positions of leadership on the Rainier committee.

After meeting with congressional representatives from Washington State in December of 1912, the Rainier committee appointed Samuel C. Lancaster, an experienced road engineer, as its special commissioner for the duration of the congressional session. Although Lancaster's engineering experience was a definite asset, the real reason for his selection was his knowledge of the nation's capital;

Rotary Club "Mt. Tacoma Trip," August 25-26, 1911. *Photo by R. R. Raymoth. Courtesy Washington State Historical Society.*

once in Washington, D.C., he quickly renewed old friendships and established contacts with high-ranking government officials. At times the work exhausted him, yet he rather enjoyed the busy schedule of dinners, lectures, and discussions. Periodically, he reported to the Rainier committee that signs were encouraging. Finally, in January of 1913, he successfully arranged a meeting with President William Howard Taft. Although Lancaster and the Rainier committee did not get all the funding they had hoped for, in 1914 the park's annual appropriation did increase.

Meanwhile, the media had discovered Mount

Rainier. The park's publicity program, in large part developed by the Rainier committee, was clearly paying off. Park information found its way into feature newspaper articles, conservation magazines, photograph and souvenir albums, descriptive books (such as *The Mountain That Was "God,"* by John H. Williams), and railroad advertising. In November 1915 the park received further national attention when the *Saturday Evening Post* published a lengthy article describing Rainier and its needs.

Nor was this all. For years the Interior Department had groped for a plan to administer all of the national parks. The parks desperately needed coordination to implement uniform policies and work out common problems. A major step toward this goal came in December 1914, when Stephen T. Mather, a wealthy and energetic Californian, was appointed assistant secretary of the interior in charge of national parks. Together with Mark Daniels, general superintendent of national parks, Mather campaigned to make the parks better known and more accessible. For example, in 1915 he and his associates released the *National Parks Portfolio,* a stunning publicity volume with illustrations and descriptions of each of the major preserves. It was the first time anything of its type had been made available to the general public; indeed, the *Portfolio* was a resounding success.

Inside Mount Rainier proper, the long-awaited opening of the Paradise Valley road and completion

Rest break on road to Mount Rainier from Tacoma. Rotary Club "Mt. Tacoma Trip," August 25-26, 1911. *Photo by R. R. Raymoth. Courtesy Washington State Historical Society.*

Cover of a brochure distributed by the Tacoma Eastern Railroad, circa 1911. *Courtesy University of Washington.*

of the round-the-mountain Wonderland Trail were memorable occasions. On June 20, 1915, automobiles began climbing from Nisqually Crossing up to Ricksecker Point, their drivers and passengers thrilled by the spectacular scenery. A canyon wall rose sharply to their left; on their right an awesome cliff of several hundred feet dropped off to the Nisqually River below. At Ricksecker Point everyone paused to enjoy the magnificent view, a panorama including the mountain itself, the canyon floor, the imposing Tatoosh Range (featuring the rugged beauty of Eagle and Pinnacle peaks), and the Paradise River at the bottom of the range. From that stopping point the cars chugged up the road to Canyon Rim, where another grand view of the Nisqually Glacier and the mountain awaited them. Then it was on to Narada Falls, where the Paradise River plunges 168 feet to the rocks below. To be sure, tourists were hard pressed to describe each scene in unused superlatives.

From Narada Falls the automobiles wound their way around numerous curves, climbing every inch until the huge amphitheater of Paradise Valley suddenly came into view. By now many motorists were

Tacoma Eastern Railroad brochure, circa 1912. Owned by the Milwaukee Road, Tacoma Eastern offered passenger service to Ashford, Washington, between 1904 and 1931. *Courtesy Special Collections, University of Washington Libraries.*

Reese's Camp of the Clouds below Alta Vista, upper Paradise Valley, July 29, 1912. *Photo by Asahel Curtis. Courtesy Washington State Historical Society.*

convinced they had seen the ultimate in alpine beauty—meadows, clumps of trees, wildflowers, streams, wind-swept patterns of snow, and the towering mountain above. At last tourists and their automobiles arrived at Reese's Camp of the Clouds. Some stayed overnight; many others had already inaugurated the phenomenon of the day visitor.

By the end of July, the ninety-three-mile Wonderland Trail encircling the mountain had also been completed. For years preservationists and others had urged that such a trail be built. Not only did it ease

patroling the park, but it accommodated many hikers who wished to see the grandeur of Mount Rainier well removed from civilization. In August 1915, for example, ninety members of the Mountaineers celebrated the trail's completion by hiking its entire length. For three weeks they discovered the park's outstanding wilderness attractions—glaciers, waterfalls, subalpine lakes, wildlife, fields of flowers, soaring virgin timber, and high meadows far removed from roads.

While the Mountaineers enjoyed their historic

trip, the Rainier committee and Stephen Mather of the Interior Department discussed plans for the development of tourist accommodations. Meeting in Tacoma, they agreed that future facilities, if such were to be first class, ought to be financed by private capital and assured of long-range operating permits. In other words, Mather proposed a regulated monopoly. If only one company operated all the concessions within the park, there would be special incentive to undertake the substantial investment required. Otherwise, companies would face continual cutthroat competition in addition to the insecurity of short-term permits.

Anticipating congressional approval of the National Park Service, Mather implemented uniform policies for concessions throughout the parks as a vital step toward working out common problems. Accordingly, he challenged the business community in Washington State to form a company with local capital and leadership to coordinate and operate all concessions in Rainier. If no one responded, he warned in conclusion, he would be forced to bring in outside assistance himself.

Results, however, were speedily forthcoming. Not long after Mather's challenge, the Rainier National Park Company was formed, capitalized at $200,000. Operations were to begin as early as 1916. Delighted by the response, the Interior Department granted the organization a long-term preferential contract. Existing concessionaires, some of whom

Arriving at Paradise Inn, July 18, 1921. *Photo by Asahel Curtis. Courtesy Washington State Historical Society.*

had operated since the 1890s, reluctantly agreed to sell their facilities to the new company. In turn, it planned either to run the establishments or phase them out if they were obsolete. Among its grandiose plans was a permanent hotel, Paradise Inn, to replace Reese's Camp of the Clouds. That thirty to forty thousand visitors now entered the park during a single season more than justified the new construction. Once again, economic reality won the day; the road to Paradise had ushered in a new era indeed.

THE
NATIONAL PARK
SERVICE

On August 25, 1916, Congress established the National Park Service under the jurisdiction of the Interior Department. As expected, Stephen T. Mather was appointed director; his capable subordinate, Horace Albright, became assistant director. In the years that followed, Mather and Albright laid the foundations of an enduring park system. As one of the earlier parks, Mount Rainier was especially important as a testing ground for new ideas. For example, formation of the Rainier National Park Company represented one of the first attempts to overhaul national park concessions system wide.

On July 1, 1917, the company opened the doors of Paradise Inn. Capitalized at $100,000, the impressive structure featured a rustic lobby, dining hall, gift shops, and observation deck, all supported by great logs cut from Silver Forest. This hotel—the first permanent building constructed in the mile-high valley—clearly marked a new era in the history of Mount Rainier National Park. Thereafter, the picturesque hotel attracted thousands of overnight tourists every year. Both the park company and the park service responded to greater visitation at Paradise with still more construction and services. By 1922 a one hundred–room annex to Paradise Inn,

Auto caravan at Paradise Inn, n.d. *Photo by Asahel Curtis. Courtesy University of Washington.*

Main lobby, Paradise Inn, n.d. *Courtesy Burlington Northern Railroad.*

a guide service building, and a new electrical plant had been built. In addition, annual attractions such as ski tournaments and "tin pants" sliding—one of the most popular and lasting events—were introduced.

Travel publicity generated by the western states and the National Park Service further attracted tourists to Paradise. Locally, businessmen helped the cause by advertising Mount Rainier in their establishments. The park company itself spent thousands of dollars on colorfully illustrated material, promoting the start of each summer season with public dinners, dancing, radio concerts, and parades. Similarly, famous guests of Paradise Inn, such as John D. Rockefeller Jr., in 1921, generated even more publicity for the park.

The park service itself was still under heavy pressure to provide better public access. By the 1920s, railroads and automobiles carried millions of travelers across the nation in a never-ending search for the great outdoors. At Rainier, the focus was still the road to Paradise. The park service supported greater development, and for that reason generally approved company plans to accommodate more tourists at Longmire Springs and Paradise Valley.

Growing interest in winter sports, for example, prompted the park company to construct a one thousand–foot toboggan run near the present Longmire parking area. That facility, built during the winter of 1923–24, plus skiing and snowshoeing,

"Coasting" on snowfields above Paradise Inn, n.d. *Photo by Asahel Curtis. Courtesy University of Washington.*

drew more than 10,000 people over a period of several weeks. Expansion of winter sports facilities soon shifted to Paradise Valley, where, during the 1930s, the concessionaire attempted to make the valley the Winter Capital of the Northwest. The park service agreed to clear snow from the road to Paradise Valley, provided the company would keep Paradise Inn open beginning with the 1935–36 winter season. Olympic tryouts, an annual Winter Sports Carnival, the Silver Ski Championships (sponsored by the *Seattle Post-Intelligencer*), and the 1935 National Ski Championships, helped attract

Tacoma Eastern Railroad brochure, circa 1912. *Courtesy Special Collections, University of Washington Libraries.*

Rainier National Park Company brochure, circa 1925. *Courtesy Special Collections, University of Washington Libraries.*

thousands of skiers and other visitors to the park. During the 1939–40 season, over 100,000 people streamed to Rainier for winter recreation, and the following winter, the number surged to over 136,000.

Despite the glamour of such developments, however the park company still lost money. Even before the 1930s, it realized winter sports were primarily weekend attractions. Moreover, frequent winter storms occasionally discouraged skiers from making the trip to Paradise; growing complaints from skiers about inadequate facilities—particularly no permanent ski lift—further undermined the attractiveness of Paradise Valley. Ironically, the park service wanted the ski lift constructed, but the company could not raise sufficient funds. With the outbreak of World War II, the dream was all but dead that Paradise Valley might become a mecca for winter sports.

Meanwhile, the park service turned to the task of making Mount Rainier accessible from every side. Like the completed Wonderland Trail, connecting roads planned during the 1920s were to encircle the mountain within the park, providing access to state and county highways from all four corners. The opposition of conservationists, however, coupled with a deepening depression after 1929, forced the park service to abandon the Wonderland Road beyond sections already begun as of 1931. Instead, the park service declared the entire north side of the park be-

Young skier above Paradise Inn, 1917. *Photo by Asahel Curtis. Courtesy Washington State Historical Society.*

tween Carbon River and Yakima Park a roadless area. As funds became even more scarce, remaining road construction slowed, then stopped entirely. The West Side Road ended after fifteen miles; similarly, the Stevens Canyon link was not finished until 1957.

The construction of tourist facilities, another

Climbers with skis and snowshoes above Paradise, February 10, 1924. *Photo by Asahel Curtis. Courtesy Washington State Historical Society.*

priority since 1916, culminated its first phase in 1931, when the park company opened 500 cabins and new lodge buildings at Paradise and Yakima Park, and, to the horror of preservationists, the Paradise Golf Course—the first in any national park. Fortunately, late melting snow, frequent cold, and foggy weather combined to make golfing at Paradise impractical, ending the novel experiment after a brief period. The park service also gave the concessionaire permission to experiment with swimming and boating on icy Reflection Lake, but denied a proposal to have tree-chopping and log-rolling contests, contending that such contests are "just a bit out of place in a national park." These and other bizarre attempts to attract tourists were examples of the park company's continuing efforts to ease its financial problems, problems caused by a sharp decline in out-of-state travel to the park. Paul Sceva, who became general manager in 1929, defended the strategy as necessary and harmless. Still, from the government's point of view, the park company must restrain itself, even in the promotion of tourism.

Resource protection remained uppermost among park service obligations, and in his long tenure (1923–41) as superintendent of Mount Rainier, "Major" O. A. Tomlinson never lost sight of that mission. Outstanding examples of resource protection during his term included boundary extensions in 1926 and 1931, and the work of the Civilian Con-servation Corps. The first additions provided better protection of the Carbon and Nisqually river systems, and on January 31, 1931, Congress added fifty-three square miles (about 34,000 acres) of virgin forest lands to the park's eastern boundary, extending it to the crest of the Cascade Range. For years considerable resistance from the forest service and local economic interests had stalled congressional legislation on the matter. Horace Albright, who became director of the National Park Service in 1929 (Mather died in 1930), defended the extension as crucial to the future of the park. "No park boundary revision project now under consideration by the National Park Service," he noted, "has more merit or is of greater importance than the one covered by this legislation." The eastern addition, incidentally, included the small Ohanapecosh Hot Springs Resort, which operated independently of the park company until it closed in 1960.

Less than two months later, the federal government took another significant step in the protection of Mount Rainier and its resources. By executive order, on March 24, 1931, Secretary of Agriculture Arthur M. Hyde designated two strips of scenic forest lands totaling fifty miles in length and a half mile wide on either side of the Naches Highway as the Mather Memorial Parkway. Immediately, Interior Secretary Ray Lyman Wilbur, at the urging of Horace Albright, also proclaimed the twelve-mile

H. A. Rhodes, O. A. Tom-
linson, and Stephen Mather
looking over plans for site of
Sunrise Lodge, Yakima Park,
July 9, 1928. *Photo by Asahel
Curtis. Courtesy Washington
State Historical Society.*

section passing through the northeast corner of the park, originally known as the Cascade Parkway, as part of the same memorial.

Further boundary studies made by the park service in the 1930s and 1940s addressed the feasibility of including more national forest lands in the park to enhance wildlife protection. In April of 1945, however, Superintendent John C. Preston reported that further additions to the park were unlikely, given

the extent of logging operations outside the preserve to the north and west. Not long afterward, relentless logging on the south side of the park removed the possibility of a boundary extension there as well.

In terms of overall park protection, including projects designed to promote the appropriate use of resources, nothing in the history of Mount Rainier National Park surpassed the work of the Civilian Conservation Corps established by Franklin D.

Sunrise Lodge and cabins, Yakima Park, August 24, 1932. *Photo by Asahel Curtis. Courtesy Washington State Historical Society.*

Roosevelt and Congress early in 1933. By 1935, 500,000 young men between the ages of 18 and 25 had been assigned to 2,500 camps in national forests and parks to help prevent soil erosion, build flood control projects, aid reforestation, and erect roads and bridges. In addition, Civilian Conservation Corps projects included trail and campground construction.

At Mount Rainier there were five camps, each with approximately two hundred men, organized under the joint supervision of the U.S. Army and National Park Service during the summer of 1933. Most of the "tree soldiers" were from Chicago and New York; each made $30 per month in addition to room and board provided by the federal government. A sixth camp was established in 1934 and two more in 1938. Throughout the CCC era (1933–41), hundreds of miles of trail were maintained, con-

Picnic at Lake Tipsoo on Naches Pass Highway, September 13, 1927. *Photo by Asahel Curtis. Courtesy Washington State Historical Society.*

structed, or reconstructed in the park; entrance gateways, telephone and power lines, river-cribbing for flood control, disease and insect abatement programs, as well as patrol cabins and fire lookouts, were either built or maintained by the CCC. Overall, the CCC program in the park, as in other national parks, rendered vital resource protection while providing new recreational opportunities for a generation of Americans.

As one might expect, World War II brought serious curtailments of operations throughout the national park system. At war's end, however, American vacationers crowded the highways in record-breaking numbers. Most of them included the national parks in their travel plans. Almost a half-million visitors traveled to Mount Ranier in 1946, a record that was only to be broken with each passing year. Once again the park's facilities could not keep pace with the demand. Roads, trails, cabins, campgrounds, and government housing had fallen into disrepair. Worse, almost all the national parks were understaffed because of meager appropriations from Congress. In short, there was a national park crisis.

In 1947 Interior Secretary Julius Krug singled out Mount Rainier National Park as a prime example of the problems in the park system. Two years later, as Mount Rainier celebrated its fiftieth park anniversary, the local press used the occasion to criticize the park service and Congress for allowing the deterioration to continue. Critics around the country included the historian and journalist Bernard De Voto who, in a 1953 issue of *Harper's Magazine,* condemned Congress for allowing the national parks to be so mismanaged. Rather than endure the embarrassment, he concluded, Congress should close the parks.

Instead, Congress responded to a comprehensive park service plan to save the preserves. Known as Mission 66, the ten-year, billion-dollar program proposed to upgrade the national parks by 1966 without impairing their scenic, natural, and historic values. The park service singled out none other than Rainier as its "pilot park." New public facilities

Mount Rainier from Stevens Canyon Road. Southeast side of the mountain as seen approaching Paradise. Kautz, Wilson, and Nisqually glaciers may be seen with the long Success Cleaver on the left horizon. *Photo by Ross Bender, 1954. Courtesy National Park Service.*

(campgrounds, picnic areas, and visitor centers), completion of the long-awaited Stevens Canyon Road, linking Paradise Valley with the east side, and the relocation of park headquarters were some of the goals accomplished.

Nonetheless, the park service ignited an intense public controversy when it announced that Paradise Inn would be torn down and replaced with night lodging outside park boundaries. Paradise Valley, the service argued, not only had reached the saturation point, but the needs of park visitors had changed substantially since the inn first opened in 1917. Initially, a journey to the mountain required more than a day; accordingly, most visitors needed the overnight facilities. Modern highways and automobiles had created the phenomenon of the day visitor, the traveler who could easily make a round trip between Seattle or Tacoma and Paradise in a few hours. Thus, the park service maintained, there was no longer a need for hotel facilities at high elevations, where heavy concentrations of people were difficult to control.

All the arguments in the world, however, could not overcome the fact that Paradise Inn was a sentimental favorite of numerous park visitors. It symbolized a deeply popular tradition, and its nostalgic defenders—mostly local people who seldom stayed there—were prepared to fight the park service's decision. As the controversy heightened, the park service accepted an offer from the Rockefeller Foundation to study the question of public facilities at Mount Rainier. Completed in 1958, the survey concluded that a new hotel should be built at Paradise without other major developments; Washington State Senators Henry Jackson and Warren Magnuson immediately endorsed that recommendation.

The park service stuck to its position: the real issue was resource protection. Natural environments at Paradise would be destroyed if allowed to be overrun by ever-increasing numbers of people. To the critics of Mission 66, the issue was also Paradise Inn. Indeed, the controversy threatened to disrupt the program of redevelopment for the entire park. Finally, the park service backed off from its plan to raze Paradise Inn immediately, but made no promises about the structure's future. At the end of Mission 66, the controversy over the inn had virtually disappeared as concerns about wilderness protection shifted public attention to other new areas.

It was somewhat ironic that in the decade and a half following the official end of Mission 66 (1966), issues concerning public use in the national parks did not focus on buildings and roads as much as wilderness backcountry. Hiking and getting away from the comforts of hotel accommodations and parking lot conveniences became intensely popular, if not a fad, in the 1970s. Consequently, various user groups brought pressure, even lawsuits, to park service policies that either limited trail camping or prohibited it altogether in specific areas susceptible to environmental damage. The snowfields above Paradise Valley attracted most of the attention from the news media. Although forced to modify its hard line toward camping restrictions above Paradise, the park service succeeded in establishing its policy of limited use in remote areas. It is uncertain to what extent declining public enthusiasm for backpacking by the 1980s played a part.

In any event, whether tourist activity took place on trails above Paradise Inn, or in the hotel itself, it was clear to the federal government that the historical pattern of most park visitors making Paradise Valley their destination remained unchanged. Accordingly, millions of dollars were spent by the park service in the early 1980s to renovate the inn, thus demonstrating a commitment to the preservation of the national historic landmark. Overall, for the park service, Paradise Valley had become one of the outstanding examples in the system challenging resource protection policies.

Paradise Inn with Tatoosh Range in background, circa 1950. *Courtesy National Park Service.*

WILDERNESS IN JEOPARDY

Mount Rainier and other early national parks, noted Michael Frome in *Battle for the Wilderness,* began as "reservoirs of true wilderness." The intention was clear: to preserve these areas permanently, to allow natural forces to continue with minimum human interference, and to create public awareness that these are treasures of the national heritage. Remarkably, these lofty purposes have been largely fulfilled. The first national parks remain outstanding examples of the natural western landscape.

Campsite near Mystic Lake on north side of Mount Rainier, 1917. *Photo by Asahel Curtis. Courtesy Washington State Historical Society.*

Almost every national park, however, has had a precarious existence. In most cases, original environments have been altered to accommodate protectionist policies and recreational demands. Mount Rainier's status as a national park was settled in 1899, but road and trail construction opened remote areas. Similarly, hotels—Paradise Inn being the notable example—attracted overnight visitors, and park boundaries created artificial limits to natural habitats. Such "basic developments" were considered necessary by almost everyone for the sake of public access; the intrusions on the resource were seen as a small sacrifice.

Throughout the course of the twentieth century, it became clear that the park's wildness was far more vulnerable than its early defenders assumed. Private and federal lands on the borders of the park have been crisscrossed with logging roads and stripped of timber to the extent that park wildlife patterns have been affected. For example, elk herds grazing on clear-cut areas outside the park have grown larger and may be upsetting the ecological balance on their summer range inside the park. Moreover, decades of logging practices on adjacent lands have eliminated any possibility of further boundary extensions, although four designated wilderness areas on forest service land provide a measure of protection.

Possibly the most serious long-range threat to the park's resource is air pollution. Concentrations of arsenic have been found in vegetation, and the danger of sulphur dioxide and acid rain damage cannot be dismissed. The continuous photochemical reactions to automobile exhaust gases, in particular, create what is commonly known as smog, not to be confused with the natural haze often seen in mountainous areas. The chief concern of the park service is ozone damage to high-elevation trees and plant life at Rainier, and the worst of it is that jet airstreams can carry the polluted air to the park from great distances.

Within the park, traditional patterns of visitation remain constant. The road to Paradise Valley is still the most heavily traveled, overwhelmingly so. Because of tourist overuse, fragile subalpine meadows encircling the historic inn will probably never be restored to their original condition. Most mountain climbers—thousands each year—leave from and return to Paradise parking lots; the popularity of climbing Mount Rainier only complicates the problem of waste on the mountain itself. On a given weekend during the summer months, tourists equal in number to the population of a small city can congregate at Paradise and create urbanlike congestion. Attempts by the park service to diffuse visitor use to other sections of the park have been only moderately successful. Furthermore, in recent years the park service at Mount Rainier has learned there are limits to change; competing recreational interests have forced modification and even abandonment of policies designed to lessen environmental impact. But when the park service attempts to accommodate all conflicting demands on resource use, it courts the danger of implementing inappropriate or ill-advised regulations. "Agency impact," commented a Mount Rainier official, "can also be a threat to the park."

Nevertheless, the prospects are not unrealistic for Mount Rainier to enter its second century as a national park without further inroads on its natural landscape. From a management point of view, the park service has come of age. The resource is no longer simply observed and guarded; instead, data-based research and planning are used to formulate policies designed either to control or prevent various kinds of park damage. In recent years damaged areas have been restored to natural growth, horse and snowmobile travel restricted, and limits

Aerial view of Mount Rainier's summit. Left, Point Success (14,150 ft.); center, Columbia Crest (14,410 ft.); right, Liberty Cap (14,112 ft.). Steam still escapes from the crater's rim, where climbers rest before starting the long descent. *Photo by Bob and Ira Spring, 1972.*

imposed on backcountry camping. These examples of internal zoning have counterparts outside park boundaries where federal, state, and county agencies are cooperating to establish waterway (Nisqually River) and greenbelt zones.

Signs of an emerging public land ethic may be Mount Rainier's strongest ally. Historically, the people of the Pacific Northwest have cared for the land. Accordingly, despite economic pressures to exploit natural resources, concerned residents have insisted on preservation. Environmental education appears to be strengthening that determination, and the beneficiaries will be future generations.

A NOTE
ON THE SOURCES

The bulk of the primary sources containing information on Mount Rainier National Park is found in regional collections: University of Washington Archives, Suzzallo Library, Seattle; Washington State Historical Society, Tacoma; Nisqually Plains Room, Pacific Lutheran University, Tacoma; Record Groups 79 of the National Archives, Federal Records Center, Seattle; Park Headquarters, Mount Rainier National Park, Ashford, Washington; and Washington State University Archives, Holland Library, Pullman, Washington. In addition, the most valuable reference to Mount Rainier in re-

lation to other parks in recent times is U.S. Department of the Interior, National Park Service, *Status of the Parks, 1980: A Report to Congress* (Washington, D.C.: National Park Service, 1980). Current records are kept at the National Park Service, Pacific Northwest Region (headquarters) in Seattle.

Useful newspaper articles on the park are found in the Northwest Room, Tacoma Public Library, as well as in the files of the Washington State Historical Society and the University of Washington. The most complete historical photograph collection on Mount Rainier is the Asahel Curtis Collection, Washington State Historical Society.

For the larger framework of national park history the following provide excellent background

On the road to Paradise, n.d. *Photo by Asahel Curtis. Courtesy University of Washington.*

and context information: Alfred Runte's *National Parks: The American Experience* (Lincoln and London: University of Nebraska Press, 1979); Robert Shankland's *Steve Mather of the National Parks* (New York: Alfred A. Knopf, 1970); and Donald C. Swain's *Wilderness Defender: Horace M. Albright and Conservation* (Chicago: University of Chicago Press, 1970).

In addition, Roderick Nash is the recognized authority on changing perceptions of wilderness in American history as discussed in *Wilderness and the American Mind,* 3rd ed. (New Haven: Yale University Press, 1982).

A wide range of descriptive and interpretive articles on Mount Rainier can be found in various publications including *National Parks Magazine, The American Alpine Journal, The Mountaineer, National Geographic, Mazama,* and *Forest History.*

The most thorough study of the historic name controversy is Genevieve McCoy's "Call It Mount Tacoma: A History of the Controversy Over the Name of Mount Rainier," (M.A. thesis, University of Washington, 1984). Also, for an interpretive administrative history of the park, there is Arthur D. Martinson's "Mountain in the Sky: A History of Mount Rainier National Park," (Ph.D. dissertation, Washington State University, 1966).

For the climbing history of Mount Rainier, see Aubrey Haines, *Mountain Fever* (Portland: Oregon Historical Society, 1962); and Dee Molenaar, *The Challenge of Mount Rainier,* 3rd ed. (Seattle: The Mountaineers, 1979).

Finally, Erwin N. Thompson's "Mount Rainier National Park, Washington: Historical Resource Study, 1981," printed by the Denver Service Center, National Park Service, is an excellent reference to recent cultural resource management objectives at Mount Rainier National Park.

 ART MARTINSON is a native of Washington State and a professor of history at Pacific Lutheran University in Tacoma. He is actively involved in many academic pursuits including public history, western history, and serves as director for the Cooperative Education program at PLU. He has traveled the American West extensively and his interest in national park history reaches back to 1953 when he worked his first summer job as a trailman at Mount Rainier National Park. His articles about Mount Rainier have been published in *Forest History* and *The American West*.

WESTERN HORIZONS
Vignettes of the western experience

Also in this series

TRAINS OF DISCOVERY
Western Railroads and the National Parks
by Alfred Runte

Historical photographs and a well-researched text demonstrate the ways in which the western railroads assisted in the preservation of some of the most spectacular scenery in the West.

96 pages · 66 photos · ISBN 0-87358-349-3 · sc · $9.95

THE INTIMATE GRAND: Inside Arizona's Grand Canyon
Text by Dowling Campbell, Photographs by Mark Jefferson

Two Arizonans explore the intimate reaches of the Grand Canyon by river and trail, revealing lush natural hideaways and a bit of canyon history.

72 pages · 40 color photos · ISBN 0-87358-373-6 · sc · $8.95

MINIATURE FLOWERS: A Desert Search
Text and photographs by Robert I. Gilbreath

These delicate flowers measure approximately four millimeters in diameter and have unusual adaptations that enable them to survive harsh desert conditions. The author's journal chronicles his search for the elusive jewels of the desert.

84 pages · 35 color photos · ISBN 0-87358-382-5 · sc · $9.95

IN THE PATH OF THE GRIZZLY
Text and photographs by Alan Carey

A photographic record of the grizzly is combined with the author's observations on the bears' behavior for an insightful glimpse into grizzly life.

84 pages · 35 color photos · ISBN 0-87358-394-9 · sc · $11.95